TO BE A MARTYR

The logic behind the Shahada – a case study – the State of Israel

Tel: +97254-8030648

Email Address: kobimnsil@gmail.com

Website: www.kobisha.com

ABOUT THE AUTHOR

Kobi Shashoua is an author and a lecturer. Among his books you can find the most comprehensive book that exists to date bout the Israeli-Palestinian conflict "Israel: the truth, the whole truth and nothing but the truth." This book leads the reader chapter by chapter through the complex reality of the conflict and dissects the causes for the crisis, uncovers to the reader the true faces of the parties involved, and presents the tactics, the strategies and the true objectives, that lie below the surface. The author also wrote the book series: "Understanding the Middle East".The book you are holding in your hands is from that series.

The author, who resides in Israel, which is located in the most dangerous neighborhood of the world, in the heart of the Middle East, shares with us the facts together with the insights and the unique understanding of the region where he lives. We invite you to take part in this journey from a safe distance.

So what motivates a person to commit a suicide attack and to consciously explode into thousands of pieces? What motivates a person to try and take with him innocent people? At first glance it seems as a totally irrational thing.

Shahid, Jihad are concepts that have recently entered the public discourse, the mainstream. If until a few years ago these concepts seemed far in the eyes of Western man, things that are relevant to the Middle East, in the second half of the second decade of the second millennium it seems that the Middle East is everywhere. The huge waves of refugees flooding Europe will change its character forever. Into these waves of refugees extremist and shady forces have infiltrated with the goal to fight the Jewish and the Christians infidels. A religious war has its own logic. Sanctity of life of Western man is conceived as a weakness while death in a war against the infidels is martyrdom, a death that entails for the devout believer, the Shahid, prizes that are awarded to the brave ones, and all that, of course, with the encouragement of Allah and his representatives who are in the mosques, in the houses of worship.

Thus the logic of a religious war turns into illogic, and the sanctity of life turns into the sanctity of death and peace turns into a derogatory word. In this war there are no compromises and the soldiers.....their place in paradise is guaranteed.

The purpose of the book is to open your eyes that view our cruel world through pink glasses and to see the other reality, a reality that is anything but a reality. In the chapter we will examine the concept of "to be a Shahid".

"To be a Shahid" is the highest aspiration of many children in the Palestinian street and in the Muslim world, encouraged by educational authorities and by key figures who sanctify death.

Since suicide bombers, or Shahids, are part of the local scenery where I live in the State of Israel, I shall base my writing in this book on the enormous experience we have accumulated per force during Israel`s war against terror. Many examples will be related to the use of Shahids against the Jews in the State of Israel, but eventually you will have to internalize and to understand that this is the same war of the believers against the infidels. This is not a war over territory, this is not a war for justice this is purely a religious war and Israel is a microcosm of the processes that started to trickle to the Western world as well that is watching helplessly how the aggressive and uncompromising conflict in the Middle East enters into their homes. This is an inevitable process that stems from the desire of the believers to impose Islam on all the non-believers in the world!

MAKES NO SENSE!

In 2010 a new version of the movie "The Karate Kid" was released. The original movie has a warm place in my heart. The original movie taught us about the power of determination, about dedication and about maturity. Karate is a way of life, and whoever adopts it is expected to get valuable gifts: determination, self confidence, faith in oneself, self discipline, restrain and recognition of your abilities, a toolbox that whoever carries it is lucky.

As in the study of karate, the element of determination in the life of a Shahid is great, the dedication to Allah is total, and the profits are huge. But unlike the world of karate, the catharsis and the condition for happiness lies in the ability to explode among as many people as possible. If they are Jews, the value of the Shahid in the eyes of God increases, and if by chance they are Israelis, then you have won the jackpot! Beyond making the Shahid the darling of the merciful and compassionate God, he also gets a supply of 72 virgins with whom he can do whatever he wishes. If so, the conclusion is that each day on earth is a wasted, pointless day. Clearly then, whence comes the passion of the Shahid to blow himself up among innocent bystanders. So in the name of Allah, let us press the button.

But what actually is a Shahid?

The term Shahid is Religious-Muslim which means "a witness". This title is used as a honorific for a Muslim who has died fulfilling a religious commandment or in a war for religion.

The Palestinian attached this nickname to Palestinians who were killed during the intifada, and particularly to suicide bombers. The place of a Shahid in paradise is guaranteed, according to the verse in the Koran: "Think not of those who are slain in Allah`s way as dead. Nay, they live in the presence of their Lord; they rejoice in the bounty provided by Allah". (Chapter "Al Imran" verse 169). [1]

---

[1] From Wikipedia under the entry: "Shahid".

The Shahids are soldiers who carry the message of Jihad, a common and familiar term the true meaning of which is not clear to most of us. Jihad in Islam is a "religious struggle" or a "Holy War". The term has two common meanings in Islam: [2]

* An outer Jihad, usually a military effort directed against the pagans (heathen) in order to convert them to Islam. The external Jihad refers also to the war against the non-Muslims, who attack Muslims or rebel against the Muslim reign.

* An inner Jihad is directed toward the believer himself and causes him to deal with self-restraint and self-improvement. Permission to fight is awarded to those who are at war by virtue of their being oppressed, and to those who were expelled from their homes without a just cause (Chapters 39-40:22). A military struggle against foreign occupation, against oppression, or against any country that is not Islamic in the region called Dar-al-Islam (House of Islam), is considered a Jihad that according to many is the relevant Jihad today.

According to this definition, the war against the State of Israel is a Jihad and is legitimate because of its location, which is in the House of Islam. This outlook is accepted by the leaders of Iran, al-Qaeda, ISIS, Hezbollah and Hamas.

In 632, during Muhammad's last visit in Mecca, he declared and ruled that all Muslims are brothers, and must not fight each other.[3] They must fight against all other persons – until they say "There is no God but Allah".[4]

(2) From Wikipedia under the entry: "Jihad".

(3) From Wikipedia under the entry: "Muslim Brothers".

(4) Indeed, this phrase is completely implemented in Syria, Iran, Libya, Egypt etc.

Today, the Jihad is worldwide and is held under the definition of global Jihad that aims to fight against the infidels, mainly Jews and Christians. There are many who truly believe that the source of trouble and tension between the religions is the Jewish state that lies in the heart of the Islamic empire. The presence of the Jewish state, supported by the Christian United States, raises also the anger of the Muslims against the Christians. According to that logic, the disappearance of Israel will eliminate the tension and will enable to reach tranquility among the religions.

But that is just wishful thinking. In terms of global Jihad, the State of Israel is considered the "Little Satan" that is here due to the will of the "Great Satan", and the disappearance of the State of Israel will only escalate the situation, since it will be considered as a victory over the Great Satan, something that will increase the wish to complete the apocalypse, which is an all-out fight against the infidels.

The war is an all-out global war, and it is happening right now in Europe, Africa, Asia and Africa.

In the eyes of a Western beholder, and particularly the European one, it may seem like a passing fad. Since the Europeans feel guilty about the devastating consequences of World War II, they hurried to open their gates to immigrants from their past Islamic colonies, and today a surge of Muslim immigrants floods Europe, which is going to change it forever. Super-organizations of millions of members converge on the final goal, which is well and clearly defined by the way life of the Muslim Brothers: "Allah is our objective. The Prophet is our leader. The Koran is our constitution. Jihad is our way. Death for the sake of Allah is our highest wish."[5]

Yunis al-Astal, the Palestinian Member of Parliament who represents the Hamas movement, declared in a televised statement on the 11th of April, 2008 that Islam will "very soon" conquer Rome, will spread throughout Europe and then will take over the Unit

Martyrdom is the true wish of every fanatic Muslim, and the manifestation of this wish is by becoming a Shahid. In the State of Israel, prior to the construction of the separation fence, dozens of Muslims became   Shahids. They blew themselves up in busses full of children in Israelis cities, in restaurants, in coffee shops and wherever they could.

---

[5] From Wikipedia under the entry: "Muslim Brothers".

Contrary to the logic of Western man, their mothers were proud of their sons who were so highly honored by the all-merciful Allah.

I began the book with a comparison between Karate as a way of life and preparing a student to become a Shahid.

There is something to look forward to.....(AP Photo/Israeli Army/HO)

The heart's desire of many Palestinian children or Muslim children is to become a Shahid one day. Prima facie it sounds like an exaggeration, since a Western person tends to flip through the headlines, and he does not bother to think deeply or to check the endless information that is flowing to him. For him, it does not seem logical to commit suicide. [6] It never occurs to him that parents, teachers and leaders educate a whole generation of children to commit suicide by detonating an explosive belt on their body while murdering dozens of innocent passers-by. But this is reality. This is an indisputable truth. [7].

_____

[6] Unless his I-phone, for which he has been waiting for a week inside a tent at the entrance of the Apple store, was stolen..

(7) The picture of the baby dressed as a suicide bomber is a photo of a Palestinian baby wearing like an explosive belt-like device that was found during a search by IDF soldiers in a house in Hebron on June 29th 2002. See further details in Wikipedia under: "Picture of a baby dressed as a suicide bomber".   (8) From the article by Roy Nahmias, "Video clip and an Arab website for children: want to be Shahids", 22/06/2010. You can see the video on the Ynet website at the link:
http://www.ynet.co.il/articles/0,7340,L-390888,00.html

Many children in the world grow up engulfed with their parent's desire to provide them with a better life than they had. Most children have a very vague idea about their future occupation: astronaut, doctor, veterinarian etc.

How sad that the dream of Palestinian children is imposed by a cruel leadership that uses them with no moral inhibitions, unscrupulously, that implants in them the desire to be a Shahid as the highest hope.

The late Israeli Prime Minister, Golda Meir, said once regarding the way the Palestinian leadership and the Palestinian people treat their children, in the context of involving them in the conflict enforced on the State of Israel: "We could forgive the Arabs for killing our children, but we cannot forgive them for forcing us to kill their children. Peace with the Arabs will prevail when they will love their children more than they hate us."

If we seek adequately, we will be able to find many evidences of the use of children for the purpose of instilling hatred against the Jews.

One example of many was published in the Ynet website on 22.6.10: [8]

A Bahrain children's channel is broadcasting a song that encourages to become Shahids: " When we die as Shahids we will get to paradise. Without Palestine, what is the significance of our childhood?" The broadcasted video clip shows innocent children, pure souls corrupted by unscrupulous radical elements. The children in the song express their desire to become Shahids while their consciousness is unable to grasp

the significance. At this age they are like clay in the potter's hands. But the potter is despicable, who takes advantage of the children's innocence to further destruction, devastation and death in the name of a religious war.

Here is the song the children sing: [9]

"When we die as martyrs we will go to heaven. No, don't say we are young. This life has turned us into grownups. Without Palestine what meaning is there to childhood? Even if they give us the entire world it won't make us forget her, no no. My country and my blood are for her sake.

Children, you have fulfilled your religious obligation. **There is no God but Allah, and the martyr is Allah's favorite.** You have taught us the meaning of manhood. O Allah, with your mercy I shall be assisted O vital and enduring god..... Protect Islam and the Muslims O Allah, save the children of Palestine O Allah, take revenge for us O Allah answer our prayers. Amen"

Simply shocking!!!!

MAKES NO SENSE

The sublime prayer the children aspire for in the song is to die as martyrs, since this is Allah's preference. This is not a random brain-washing in a remote channel, this is a satanic propaganda, brain-washing broadcasted in the official channels of the Palestinian Authority and in the Arab and Muslim countries.

A satanic propaganda machine is assaulting the next generation of Palestinians from infancy. The Palestinian television networks are broadcasting such programs continuously in order to instill the hatred for the people living in the State of Israel also in the next generation of Palestinians.

---

(9) Allow me to venture and say that the children who sing do not comprehend its deep meaning.

Opinion leaders and Palestinian officials, who are not interested to deal with the issue   of the "Palestinian people", prefer to rid themselves of the responsibility and to create an additional generation of despair and hopelessness, and the only way to get out of it is by dying as a martyr.

The Palestinian television is working tirelessly to create pro-Palestinian propaganda (and anti-Israeli) in the language of children, so that they can know the really important things.

Another example:

A Palestinian television interviewer asks Palestinian girls aged eleven about their wishes when they grow up:

The interviewer: "You spoke about the Shahada as a beautiful thing. Do you think it is a beautiful thing?"

"The Shahada is a very beautiful thing. Everybody yearns for Shahada. What could be better than to get to paradise?"

The interviewer: "What is preferable, peace with full rights for the Palestinian people or Shahada?"

"The Shahada. I will get my rights after I become a Shahid, because we will not remain children forever".

The interviewer: "Ok, Yusra, do you agree with these things?"

"The Shahada is obviously a good thing, because we don't want this world but the afterlife. What will be useful to us is not this world but the afterlife, therefore Palestinian teenagers are not like any other teenagers, they are hot blooded, and of course they prefer Shahada, because they are Palestinians. The children of Palestine adopted the idea that this is Shahada and that death in Shahada is a very good thing.

Every Palestinian child, let's say aged 12, says: "God, grant me a Shahada". [10]

---

(10) You can watch the video in the website: http://pilots-wives.nana10.co.il/Article/?ArticlesID=612459&

The answers leave no room for doubts and all I have to say is

MAKES NO SENSE!

Beyond that the matter is terrifying, more annoying is the question that the interviewer asked: What is preferable, peace or to be a Shahid. The decisive answer given by the girl illustrates to what extent hatred is already rooted, and how difficult it would be "to sell" the idea of peace to the new generation of Palestinians.

The desire to be a Shahid encompasses the whole radical Islam, and is not owned by the Palestinians only.

In the World Trade Center disaster, on September 11th, 2001, 2,974 workers, citizens and passers-by lost their lives. Together with them 19 Shihads were killed. In the "Peace flotilla" to the Gaza Strip (May 2010) at least 4 "peace activists" were aboard the boat Marmara who became Shahids. [11] Suicide bombings are happening all the time, in (partial list) Spain, England, Iraq, Afghanistan, India. The supply of virgins is running out.....Control yourselves a bit for God's sake!

(11) http://www.jihadwatch.org/2010/06/three-of-four-turks-killed-in-jihad-flotilla-raid-had-declared-desire-for-islamic-martyrdom-another.html

The use of suicide bombers has many advantages for those who send them, for the Shahid and for his family.

The advantages of a suicide attack for the terror organization:

1. Maximum victims and maximum damage.
2. The method ensures that the attack is performed in perfect timing with having   maximum people within the range of the attack.
3. Maximum media coverage.
4. It is almost impossible to stop a suicide bomber and withhold the attack once he is already on his way to the target.
5. No need to plan an escape route.
6. The terrorist does not survive, and therefore it is impossible to interrogate him   about those who sent him.

The advantages for the suicide bomber:

1. The social status of the Shahid and of his family soars sky-high.
2. In addition to being honored, his family gets also a financial bonus – that amounts mostly to thousands of dollars.
3. In addition, the Shahid gets a huge personal reward: eternal life in paradise, permission to see Allah`s face, 72 virgin maidens, guaranteed eternal life in heaven also for 70 of his family members.

The reward for the action of the suicide boomer is therefore enormous – nationally, religiously, socially, financially and personally. No wonder the Hamas and the Islamic Jihad find volunteers easily because the believers stand in line! [12]

Following is a summary of hundreds of suicide bombing attacks committed in Israel by Shahids from among the "Palestinian people" that profess to be "peace seeking people" between the years 1993-2008:

(12) The list of benefits is taken from:
http:///www.knesset.go.il.library/heb/docs/sif019.htm

Year	# of virgins provided	# of Terror Attacks	# of Victims
1993	72	1	2
1994	360	5	38
1995	288	4	40
1996	288	4	59
1997	216	3	24
1998	72	1	1
1999	144	2	0
2000	144	2	2
2001	2,520	35	85
2002	3,816	53	189
2003	1,872	26	143
2004	864	12	55
2005	576	8	25
2006	432	6	15
2007	72	1	3
2008	72	1	1
2009	0	0	0
2010	72	1	1
Total:	11,880	165	683

The data in the table are taken from reports of the Shabak [13] and from the entry "Suicide attacks in Israel" in Wikipedia. The breached border between the State of Israel and the Palestinian territories enabled many Shahids to infiltrate into

Israeli territory (and fulfill in practice their dream to shack up with the virgin maidens). Over 600 Israeli citizens were massacred; residents who were unfortunate to be by chance on the bus that was torn to a thousand pieces, who were in a restaurant celebrating, in coffee shops and in crowded places. Adults, children and babies were ripped into thousands of pieces. Today there are thousands of Israelis who suffer from various degrees of injuries, burns, torn limbs, traumas, loss of eyesight, loss of hearing, fear and anxiety. This is a terror that is directed mainly against the civilian population. Since 2011 the table is empty but not because the terror organizations have sobered up to realize that their way is wrong, God forbid. I will refer to the matter in the next paragraph.

Families were torn apart, parents lost their children and children lost their parents, their brothers, their relatives, their legs, their eyesight.

The list is still long, and no explanation and excuse can help! This is murder of the most despicable degree.

I sometimes hear ridiculous comments by people who up till recently were not a part of the conflict (the conflict has long ago broken across the walls of the Middle East on its way to become global) who justify the attacks and the murder of dozens of innocent Jewish people that live in the State of Israel as consequent to the "occupation", the "murder of the Palestinian babies by the soldiers of the Zionists occupation army" and other blood libels. Now, are these argumentations valid also in Europe? Or is it something else there – so the answer is really no! This is a religious war of the believers against the infidels. The Hamas organization, which is perceived by the European leftist elites as a freedom fighter organization, states in its Charter among other things:

"Israel will rise and will continue to exist until Islam destroys it, as it destroyed what preceded it". – A religious war undoubtedly.

"Our campaign with the Jews is great and very crucial and it requires all the truthful efforts. This is a step after which additional steps must necessarily come, a troop that needs perforce to be supported by more and more troops from the vast Islamic and Arab world, until the enemies are eradicated and the victory of Allah materializes!" Here the Jews are mentioned and not the citizens of the State of Israel. The origin of the conflict therefore is purely religious and unfortunately this war has now spread beyond the Middle East to the stronghold of the infidels. The reason for the attacks in Europe is the same as the reason for the attacks that happen in the State of Israel – the war against the infidels!

---

(13) Israel Security Agency - ISA.

Destruction, devastation and death in the suicide bombing attack on a bus in Jerusalem, 18th May 2003. Photo: flash 90.

Would you have believed that a few hours earlier the bus was overcrowded with children, babies, and innocent civilians?

MAKES NO SENSE!

The remains of the bus in line 26 that was blown up by a suicide bomber in Jerusalem on 21st August 1995. Photo: Avi Ohayon, Government Press Office.

This is how it was in at least 26 busses!

"But you deserve it" many say and justify it as consequent to the "genocide", the "massacre", the brutality of the Zionist entity. Is that so? Remember, and I repeat this over and over again, Israel is the only democracy in the Middle East. In a place that used to be some decades ago a desert, a glorious country was established, against all odds, with no natural resources, and in defiance of the enemies that surround it. This country is conducted according to law, morale and justice and constitutes a role model for many countries in the world. Controversial security events are subject to internal investigation, to conclusions and even to punishment of the culprits if there are any. The code of Purity of Arms is its guiding light.

Against whom are we fighting? Against terror organizations that regard the destruction of the State of Israel only as part of global Jihad. These organizations are using constantly their abilities in order to hurt as many Israelis as possible – Jews indiscriminately. These organizations have studied well the vulnerable points of Western man and use his mechanisms in order to strike mercilessly Israelis and Jews. They mingle with the local population and operate out of residential apartments and offices, and they wish for a response that will harm citizens in order to present it as a massacre. They use the media so efficiently, that each death of a Palestinian turns into an international event, while an attack on Israelis is played down and justified, since they are the "occupiers". An Israeli counterattack is presented as disproportionate and directed to strike civilian population. A counterattack always calls for a threat by the terrorist organizations to retaliate, and thus we get the perpetuation of the cycle of bloodshed, that will end, according to them, only when the "occupying Zionist entity" is destroyed.

MAKES NO SENSE!

The amount of terrorist attacks, mainly in 2001-2003, turned the Israelis into sitting ducks. At least 26 busses, with the passengers, have exploded. Almost every Israeli has suffered directly or indirectly from the terror. We all have friends, acquaintances or relatives that were hurt by suicide bombings, and we have all passed in places where attacks have happened. I remember myself playing in the high-school yard during recess when I saw how a primitive pipe bomb that was planted at the bottom of the bus exploded. During the Passover holiday on 17/05/2006, when I worked as an investment manager, I felt how the glass of the building were about to be torn off when I heard the echoes of the explosion of the terrorist's explosive belt 500 feet away from the office where I worked. A few minutes after the explosion a bloodcurdling silence prevailed. Only then police cars and ambulances started to get to the place to take care of the wounded. The outcome was fetal with 11 dead people and about 70 wounded, while the word "wounded" does them injustice and is unable to describe the amputees, the persons with disfigured faces and bodies, people mentally and physically crippled.

The following graph illustrates how serious the danger still is:

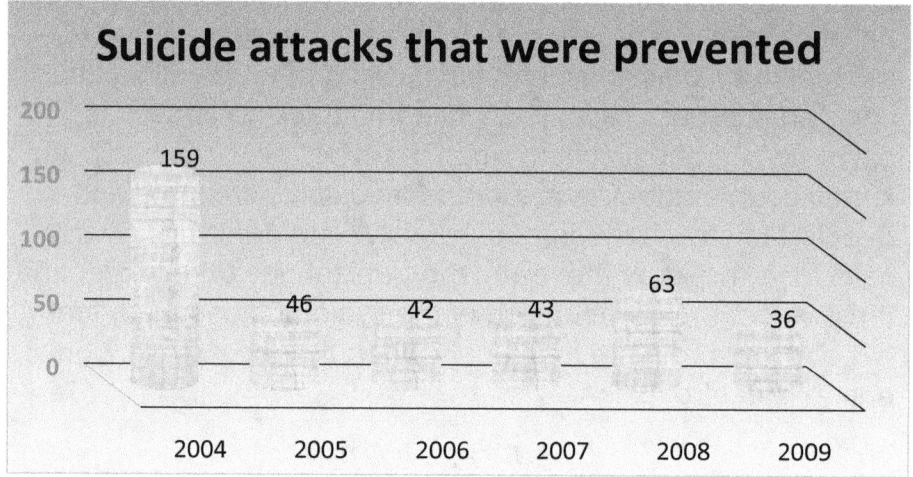

Make no mistake; the decrease in the amount of suicide attacks was not due to the disillusionment of the Palestinians. The construction of the "damned apartheid fence" separated many potential Shahids from uniting with their virgins somewhere in paradise.

The construction of the separation fence led to a dramatic drop in the amount of suicide attacks. Hamas did not stay complacent and as the famous line from the movie Jurassic Park (14) goes: – "Life will find a way". The Palestinians replaced the suicide bombers with missiles that are fired constantly on communities in the State of Israel (Hamas will find a way).

In the following graph you can see that with the decrease in the amount of suicide attacks (not as a result of lack of motivation), the amount of launchings of various missiles from the Gaza Strip toward Israeli cities has increased.

_____

(14) In the movie Jurassic park only the females were created for the purpose of controlling the reproduction but nature found a way to create also a male in order to ensure the survival of the race.

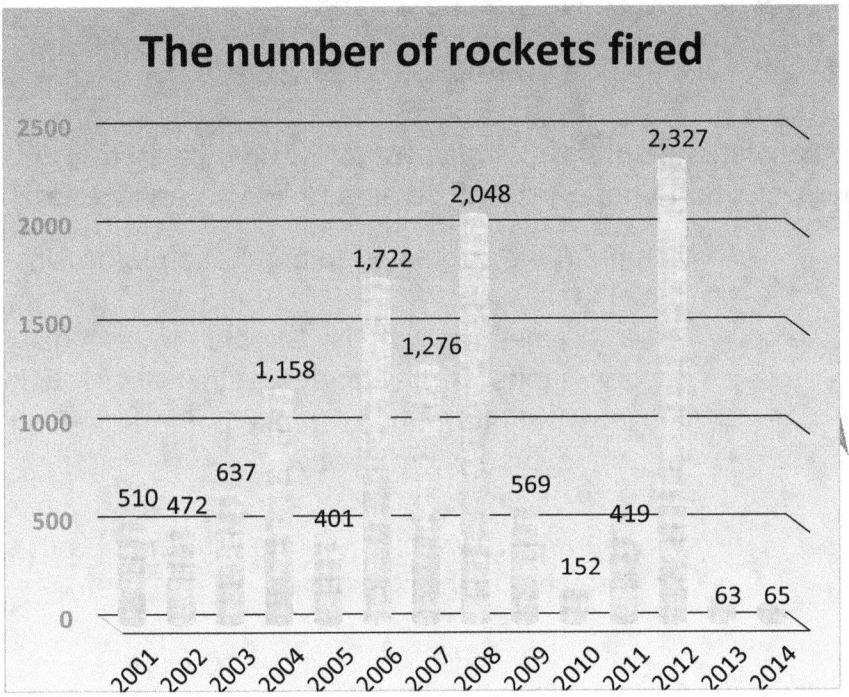

The number of rockets fired

The graph shows the number of steep trajectory gunfire attacks (15) and not the total number of missiles, which is a lot higher. Can you imagine that over 9,000 pipes heavily loaded with explosives have been fired from the Gaza Strip, aimed to wreak havoc in civilian environments, and preferably during the hours when parents take their children to school?

The decrease in 2009 is due to operation "Cast lead" (December 2008 – January 2009) during which the IDF attacked the Hamas infrastructure and forced the organization to reach an understanding with the "Zionist Entity". In this case, as well, the cease-fire was one-sided and an attempt was made to impose it by the UN Security Council (resolution 1860). This is a well-known technique: each time Israel has the upper hand, the Arab countries rush to the UN institutions to impose a cease-fire. The only time it will not be necessary, will be when they have the upper hand.

MAKES NO SENSE!

To conclude the chapter, there are a few unanswered questions that I hope you will be able to find an answer for:

- What did the virgins do to be chosen to be with the Shahid?
- After the meeting with the Shahid they are no longer virgins, what is their fate then?
- Do they get pregnant as a result of the meeting or do they use contraceptives?
- Why 72 virgins?
- While they are waiting to unite with their heart`s desire, what is their favorite song? [16]

---

[15] Shooting in an arched track that enables skipping over barriers and obstacles such as the separation fence.

[16] A hint: Madonna.

The axiom of the Shahid: the biggest worry of every Shahid is to get killed on the way to get the job done. Since the mission is suicide and it ends in death, the outcome in both cases is supposed to be identical, but it is not so, or is it?

But Good Heavens, what happens if as a result of force major or some mishap the Shahid fails to explode and to fulfill his wish to meet his 72 virgins. Even then, in fact, he "profits" adequately. The conditions of detention of such prisoners in Israeli prisons are like those in a summer camp. The prisoners enjoy many rights and they get an opportunity to acquire a reputable academic degree at the expense of the Israeli tax payer whom they were so eager to blow up. Many of these prisoners study at the Open University and are granted academic degrees for free. Prison life, as well, is easy and includes sumptuous cuisine, active social life, cell phones, family visits etc. Bear in mind, these are the most despicable people of the worst kind who believe that the infidels must be annihilated regardless of age and gender. The more the merrier, and in this situation the State of Israel decides, for some reason, to recompense those Shahids who failed in their mission.

These prisoners await a situation in which an Israeli soldier is kidnapped and is held alive or dead. The sanctity of life of the Jews who live in the State of Israel is perceived as a vulnerable point and is exploited to the most by the terror organizations that are trying constantly to kidnap soldiers and keep them alive or, if less successful, dead, because then the number of prisoners exchanged will be lower. This happened in several transactions in the past while the latest and probably the most famous one is the exchange of prisoners in which the Israeli soldier Gilad Shalit was given back.

Gilad Shalit was released from captivity on 18.11.11, after 5 and half years. His return was a day of celebration in Israel. The entire process of his release and his return to Israel were broadcasted live. The Prime Minister in person hugged him and "delivered" him to his father. But in exchange for the release the State of Israel paid a heavy price. 1,027 terrorists were released. 60% of them will return to terrorism. Many terrorists with blood of Israeli citizens on their hands were released in the transaction. There have been tremendous uncertainties, but the image of the soldier`s union with his family caused to forget the price, for a moment.

So that in the long run to be a Shahid in the State of Israel seems like a Win-Win deal. If you succeed, you become a porn star in paradise – If you fail....maximum you will get an academic degree.

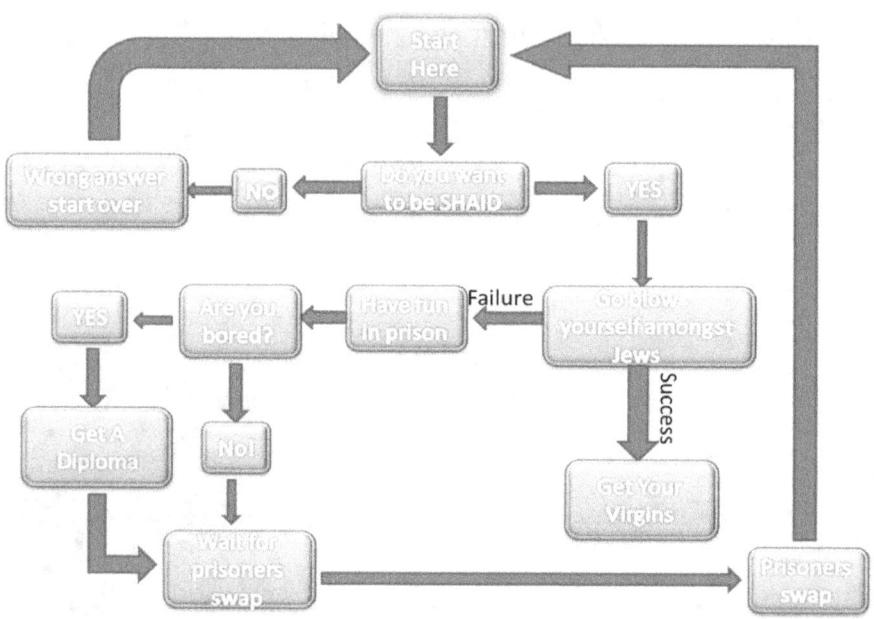

The wave of terrorist attacks in Europe wasn't conceived in a vacuum but is a direct continuation of a painful daily reality that prevails in Israel for several decades. The Shahid, the religion warrior, the holly warrior, does not hesitate to blow himself up into a thousand pieces and fragments while he wreaks havoc and death all around him. In the eyes of a Western person this is perceived as a clearly illogical thing. The sanctity of life is trampled contemptuously by the radical Islam that sanctifies and praises death as martyrdom. The reversal of these values is on a frontal collision track in Europe and is bound to cause there, unfortunately, days of sorrow, misery and grief.

This book is part of a series of books I have written about the Middle East. I made sure to write the books so that they fully exhaust the subject, are informative, and free of political correctness so that they will actually present facts and truths concerning the conflict in the Middle East with the aim to show a different angle from the one that the media and many activists show out of an agenda and worldview that ignore facts and historical truths. I hope you will find this book and other books that I have written useful and eye openers that cast a different light on the reality in the Middle East. As a writer, I would be happy to get a positive review in the book website from which this book was purchased because it would help me, with your generous help, to spread the truth to other readers who are eager to learn more about the conflict that is taking place in the Middle East.

In order to enhance the understanding of the Middle East I welcome you to deepen reading the book series I have written on this subject called: "Understanding the Middle East".

The books are available through an assigned website: www.kobisha.com

Or type "Kobi Shashoua" in the Amazon website.

You are welcome to contact me directly by e-mail: kobimnsil@gmail.com

And by phone: 972-54-8030648

Yours Truly,

Kobi Shashoua